PRAISE FOR
Leading with Purpose: Daily Affirmations for Effective Leadership

"The biggest leadership challenge for many is motivating their team and themselves. This book provides daily reminders of important leadership traits and skills that may become lost during our daily routines. A great reference for leaders, managers, and even trainers."
– G. Hickey, Technical Activities Manager, Society of Petroleum Engineers

"These leadership affirmations will be an invaluable tool for leaders at all levels, supervisory, managerial, and executive. Doctor Roessler clearly spells out the methodology needed to effectively make use of them. I expect that these affirmations will easily stand the test of time and be a valuable resource for generations of leaders, yet unborn."
– John R Emery, Retired Associate Dean, Science, Technology, Engineering, and Math (STEM), Eastfield College

"In today's dynamic and rapidly changing environment, Dr. Roessler provides leaders and those they lead the foundation to shift their mindset from being resistant to change to embracing the journey of change in a positive light. Dr. Roessler's approach to affirmations in the context of leadership is refreshing and a needed tool in a successful leader's toolbox."
– Dr. Bethany Valente, Managing Partner, Tempo7, LLC

"Whether using this guide to improve leadership skills or simply improve your outlook on life, the affirmations include valuable information and examples on how to apply it to one's life. Good leadership is a foundation to a successful work environment, and taking these affirmations to heart and applying them will certainly be helpful in creating a functional and positive environment. A must read for any level of employee!"
– Courtney MacIntyre, RN

Leading with Purpose: Daily Affirmations for Effective Leadership

Volume 2

By Dr. John E. Roessler

Leading with Purpose: Daily Affirmations for Effective Leadership

Volume 2

By Dr. John E. Roessler

First Edition

ISBN-13: 978-0-9979759-3-2

Book and Cover design by John E. Roessler

DEDICATION

To my family for your enduring support throughout my years of service to this great Nation and its people. You define me.

CONTENTS

The most important thing you can offer your team is your authentic self – be vulnerable.

HOW TO USE THIS BOOK

At the onset, I thought it important to share a few thoughts on how you may use this book in your leadership journey. Using a book on daily leadership affirmations can be a powerful way to develop your leadership skills and cultivate a positive and empowering mindset. Here are some tips on how to use this book on daily leadership affirmations effectively:

1. Set a specific goal: Before using the book, it's important to set a specific leadership goal that you want to achieve. This will help you select affirmations that are specific to your goal and keep you motivated.
2. Choose a time and place: Set aside a specific time each day to read your affirmations, such as in the morning before work or at night before bed. Find a quiet place where you can focus and reflect on the affirmations.
3. Read and reflect: Read the affirmation slowly and reflect on its meaning. Visualize yourself

embodying the qualities and actions described in the affirmation, and feel the emotions that come with being a successful leader.

4. Repeat and reinforce: Repeat the affirmation several times, either out loud or in your head. This will help reinforce the message and integrate it into your subconscious mind.

5. Take action: After reading your affirmation, identify specific actions you can take throughout the day to embody the qualities and actions described in the affirmation. This will help you turn your affirmations into actionable steps toward your leadership goal.

6. Track your progress: Keep track of your progress and the changes you see in your mindset and leadership skills. This can help you stay motivated and adjust your affirmations as needed.

7. Use the book as a reference: Use the book as a reference whenever you need a boost of inspiration or motivation. Flip through the pages and select an affirmation that resonates with you in the moment.

In summary, using a book on daily leadership affirmations can be a powerful way to develop your leadership skills and cultivate a positive and empowering mindset. Set a specific goal, choose a time and place, read and reflect, repeat and reinforce, take action, track your progress, and use the book as a reference. By incorporating daily affirmations into your leadership development, you can transform your leadership and become the best version of yourself as a leader.

PREFACE

Leadership is a process that requires a unique set of skills, knowledge, and mindset. It involves inspiring, motivating, and guiding others toward a common goal. In today's rapidly changing and uncertain world, being an effective leader is more important than ever before. However, leadership is not an easy task, and it often comes with its own set of challenges and obstacles.

One powerful tool that can help leaders navigate these challenges and overcome obstacles is the use of affirmations. Affirmations are positive statements that help you to reprogram your subconscious mind and change your thoughts and beliefs. When used correctly, affirmations can help you develop a positive and empowering mindset, increase your self-confidence, and improve your leadership skills.

This book is designed to provide you with a comprehensive guide to leadership affirmations and how to best apply them in your leadership role. In this book, you will learn how to use affirmations to:

- Build self-confidence and resilience
- Overcome limiting beliefs and self-doubt
- Improve communication skills
- Enhance creativity and innovation
- Build strong relationships with team members
- Inspire and motivate others
- Create a positive and empowering work culture

Through the use of powerful and effective affirmations, you can transform your leadership style and become the best version of yourself as a leader.

Throughout this volume, you will notice a repetitive nature or cadence that comes through – this is intentional, a means to reinforce key concepts. You will also come across themes that seem to repeat but rest assured these are nuanced and are intentionally meant to reinforce key concepts and address individual development needs. How this book is approached and ultimately used will be as unique as the leaders who apply the material to their lives. Ultimately, this book will provide you with practical strategies, tips, and techniques to help you integrate leadership principles into your daily routine and leverage their power to become a more effective and successful leader. Clear your mind, be teachable, and open yourself to exploring leadership from within.

DAILY AFFIRMATIONS

Today's Leadership Affirmation:

I foster an environment of trust and mutual respect in my team, allowing for open communication and collaboration.

I foster an environment of trust and mutual respect in my team, allowing for open communication and collaboration. This affirmation speaks to my ability to create a positive and supportive work environment where team members feel comfortable sharing their thoughts and ideas. I prioritize building trust and mutual respect among team members, which allows for open and effective communication and collaboration. I will foster an environment of trust and mutual respect in my team, allowing for open communication and collaboration. I will take active steps to build trust and establish a supportive work environment where individuals feel comfortable sharing their thoughts and ideas. I recognize the importance of trust and respect in enabling effective collaboration, and I am committed to creating an environment where these values are prioritized.

Today's Leadership Affirmation:

I value the diverse perspectives and skills of those around me and create opportunities for them to shine.

I value the diverse perspectives and skills of those around me and create opportunities for them to shine. This affirmation highlights my appreciation for the unique perspectives and talents of those around me and my desire to create opportunities for them to showcase their strengths. I will recognize and appreciate the unique talents and abilities of each individual, and work to create a supportive and inclusive environment where everyone feels valued and heard. Today, I will actively seek out and embrace the diverse perspectives and skills of those around me, creating opportunities for them to shine. I will continuously strive to make the most of the diversity within my network and collaborate with all team members, recognizing that our differences make us stronger.

Today's Leadership Affirmation:

I actively listen to and seek out the ideas and opinions of others in networking and collaboration efforts.

I actively listen to and seek out the ideas and opinions of others in networking and collaboration efforts. Actively listening and seeking out the ideas and opinions of others is essential for effective collaboration. This affirmation emphasizes the importance of being open to the perspectives of others and actively seeking out their input. I will prioritize actively listening and seeking out the ideas and opinions of others in all of my networking and collaboration efforts. I understand the value of diverse perspectives and will make a conscious effort to incorporate the thoughts and suggestions of those around me in order to achieve success.

Today's Leadership Affirmation:

I am aware of the strengths and weaknesses of my team members and utilize them to their fullest potential.

I am aware of the strengths and weaknesses of my team members and utilize them to their fullest potential. By understanding the unique skills and abilities of my team members, I am able to assign tasks and projects that are a good fit, leading to increased productivity and job satisfaction. I will offer tailored support, coaching, and training and mentorship where it's needed most. I will play to my team's strengths, encouraging collaboration and team members to complement each other's abilities, leading to innovative solutions and increased performance. Today, I will engage in one-on-one conversations with each team member, actively listening to their goals, concerns, and ideas. This action will foster a deeper understanding of their individual strengths and weaknesses and allow me to tailor assignments and support to optimize their potential leading to a more productive and successful team.

Today's Leadership Affirmation:

I provide opportunities for my team members to grow and develop, both professionally and personally.

I provide opportunities for my team members to grow and develop, both professionally and personally. This affirmation highlights the importance of providing opportunities for team members to grow and develop. By providing these opportunities, I can help team members improve their skills, advance their careers, and achieve their personal goals. By offering training, mentoring, and new responsibilities, I am committed to helping my team members achieve their full potential and build a more skilled and capable team. Today, I will actively seek out and provide opportunities for my team members to grow and develop, both professionally and personally.

Today's Leadership Affirmation:

I communicate clearly and effectively with my team members, keeping them informed and engaged.

I communicate clearly and effectively with my team members, keeping them informed and engaged. Communicating effectively and frequently, I am able to ensure that my team members are well-informed and engaged in the work we are doing. I will communicate clearly and effectively with my team members, keeping them informed and engaged. I understand the importance of effective communication in keeping team members informed and engaged in their work. Thus, today, I will build trust, foster engagement, and ensure that everyone is working toward the same goals.

Today's Leadership Affirmation:

I recognize and celebrate the accomplishments of my team members, fostering a positive and motivated work environment.

I recognize and celebrate the accomplishments of my team members, fostering a positive and motivated work environment. By recognizing and celebrating the successes of my team members, I will foster a sense of pride and enthusiasm within the team. Through this awareness, I am able to create a positive and motivated work environment, which leads to increased productivity and job satisfaction. Today, I will actively acknowledge and celebrate the achievements and successes of my team members, and I will cultivate a positive and motivated work environment where everyone feels valued and inspired. I am committed to performing these actions to not only boost morale but to contribute to higher productivity and enhanced job satisfaction among my team.

Today's Leadership Affirmation:

I am an empathetic leader, understanding the challenges and pressures my team members may be facing.

I am an empathetic leader, understanding the challenges and pressures my team members may be facing. By being empathetic, I am able to gain a deeper understanding of the challenges my team members may be facing. This approach will allow me to provide support and resources when needed. I will prioritize being an empathetic leader by being present and offering support when situations arise that impact my team members. By taking the time to listen and show understanding, I am able to provide support and resources to my team members when they need it, creating a more positive, healthy, and solution-oriented work environment. Today, I will listen fully to others and open myself to their perspectives. I will not dismiss the importance of another person's challenges or pressures at work or in their personal lives.

Today's Leadership Affirmation:

I take the time to get to know my team members on a personal level, building trust and understanding.

I take the time to get to know my team members on a personal level, building trust and understanding. By taking the time to understand my team members as individuals, I am able to create a stronger, more cohesive team and foster a positive work environment. I will take the time to get to know my team members on a personal level, building trust and understanding. By investing in understanding my team members as individuals, I can build stronger relationships, which can assist us in working together more productively, helping to overcome obstacles. Today, I will dedicate time to connect with my team more deeply. I will make room for small talk and I will share appropriate personal stories while allowing space for others to do the same.

Today's Leadership Affirmation:

I give credit where credit is due, acknowledging the hard work and accomplishments of my team members.

I give credit where credit is due, acknowledging the hard work and accomplishments of my team members. I understand the importance of actively acknowledging the hard work and accomplishments of my team members. This approach not only helps to build morale and motivation within the team, but also helps to create a culture of accountability and responsibility. I am committed to recognizing the accomplishments of my team members. I understand the importance of building morale and motivation within the team, and creating a culture of accountability and responsibility. As a leader, I actively seek out opportunities to recognize and celebrate the achievements of my team members.

Today's Leadership Affirmation:

I understand the importance of effective following in achieving success, both personally and professionally.

I understand the importance of effective following in achieving success, both personally and professionally. Following is an important aspect of any team, and I am aware of this as success can only be achieved by working together and following the lead of others. I recognize that effective following is not about blindly obeying orders, but rather about being an active and engaged member of the team, providing constructive feedback and offering solutions when necessary. The act of following another requires a level of self-awareness, empathy, and adaptability to be able to support and follow their lead while also contributing my own unique skills and abilities. I recognize that in any team, there will be individuals with different strengths, perspectives, and communication styles, and that being able to effectively follow and support these individuals is critical to the success of the team. To this end, I am committed to continuously

[12]

improving my skills in this area. I actively seek feedback from others to understand how I can better support them, and I am always willing to adapt my approach to better meet their needs.

Today's Leadership Affirmation:

I actively seek input and feedback from my team members when solving problems.

I actively seek input and feedback from my team members when solving problems. I understand that many heads are better than one, and that by collaborating with my team, I can find a more effective solution. I recognize that their perspectives and expertise can help us find the most appropriate and effective solutions. By fostering a collaborative approach, I can create a more inclusive work environment and build a sense of shared ownership in problem-solving within the team. I will actively seek input and feedback from my team members when solving problems, recognizing the value of collaboration and diverse perspectives. By doing so, I can leverage the knowledge and experience of my team, and together we can develop more effective solutions for the team and overall organization.

Today's Leadership Affirmation:

I am able to think critically and logically when faced with a problem, quickly identifying potential solutions.

I am able to think critically and logically when faced with a problem, quickly identifying potential solutions. I have the ability to analyze complex situations, break them down into smaller parts and develop a logical plan of action. I possess the skills to think critically and logically when faced with a problem, allowing me to quickly identify potential solutions. With the ability to analyze complex situations, break them down into smaller parts, and develop a logical plan of action, I am confident in my problem-solving abilities and my capacity to lead my team toward success. Today, I will apply logic when faced with challenges, I will work to identify solutions using input from my team.

Today's Leadership Affirmation:

I am responsive to the concerns and perspectives of my team members when making decisions.

I am responsive to the concerns and perspectives of my team members when making decisions. I actively listen to my team members' concerns and take them into consideration when making decisions. I understand that their perspectives are important and valuable in making the best choices for the team. I will make it a priority to listen to the concerns and perspectives of my team members when making decisions. I will create a safe and open environment for my team members to voice their opinions, and I will take their perspectives into consideration when making decisions that affect the team. By doing so, I will ensure that my decisions are informed, effective, and aligned with the needs and goals of the team.

Today's Leadership Affirmation:

I am committed to fostering a culture of continuous learning and improvement within the team.

I am committed to fostering a culture of continuous learning and improvement within the team. I believe that learning and growth are essential for success and that fostering a culture of continuous improvement is key to achieving this. I actively seek out opportunities for professional development and provide them to my team members. As a leader, I understand the importance of learning and growth and recognize that it is essential for your team's success. By prioritizing professional development and sharing those opportunities, I am setting my team up for long-term success and helping them stay ahead of industry trends. Fostering a culture of continuous improvement can help our team achieve great things together and create a supportive and positive work environment.

Today's Leadership Affirmation:

I am committed to responsible and effective fiscal stewardship, maximizing the value of financial resources.

I am committed to responsible and effective fiscal stewardship, maximizing the value of financial resources. This affirmation highlights the importance of responsible and effective financial management. By committing to responsible and effective fiscal stewardship, a leader can ensure that financial resources are being used in the most efficient and effective way possible. I will take ownership of my role in managing financial resources, and work to ensure that every expenditure is in line with our values and goals. I understand the importance of taking personal responsibility for financial management. By taking ownership of one's role in managing financial resources and ensuring that every expenditure aligns with organization values and goals, a leader can establish a culture of responsible financial stewardship.

Today's Leadership Affirmation:

I am aware of the financial impact of my decisions, and consider long-term ramifications.

I am aware of the financial impact of my decisions, and consider long-term ramifications. I understand that financial decisions can have long-term impact to the organization, and I strive to make choices that will benefit the team in the long run. I will be conscious of decisions that could affect payroll and general expenses. I will ensure I set aside funds for awards and training for my employees. I will be responsible and accountable, striving to make choices that will benefit the organization's fiscal health. I understand that financial decisions have a ripple effect, and I will consistently take into account the financial impact of my decisions on the organization's viability. By doing so, I will help ensure that the choices I make are in the best interests of the organization, both now and in the future.

Today's Leadership Affirmation:

I actively seek out and identify cost-saving opportunities, while still maintaining the integrity of operations.

As a leader, I am committed to optimizing the performance and efficiency of our organization by actively seeking out cost-saving opportunities while maintaining the integrity of our operations. I recognize the importance of balancing cost savings with quality and efficiency, and I am dedicated to achieving this balance. I understand that by identifying areas where we can save costs, we can reinvest those resources into other areas of the organization, such as research and development or employee training, to drive growth and success. I will actively seek out and identify cost-saving opportunities, while still maintaining the integrity of our operations. I will engage with my team to brainstorm and implement innovative solutions that reduce costs and enhance the performance of our organization. I will continuously analyze our operations to identify areas where we can optimize our processes and procedures to save costs and improve efficiency. Today, I will ensure that we are making the most of our resources and creating a culture of continuous improvement within our organization.

Today's Leadership Affirmation:

I encourage the use of technology and automation to reduce labor costs and increase efficiency.

I encourage the use of technology and automation to reduce labor costs and increase efficiency. I recognize that technology and automation can play a key role in reducing costs and increasing efficiency. I actively encourage the use of these tools within the organization in order to improve operations and reduce labor costs. I will actively encourage the use of technology and automation to reduce labor costs and increase efficiency within the organization. I recognize that these tools can play a key role in streamlining processes, reducing errors, and improving overall productivity. By encouraging their use, I will help create a more efficient and effective work environment, while also reducing labor costs for the organization. Through my efforts, I will help position my team for long-term financial success, while also providing a better work experience for all employees.

Today's Leadership Affirmation:

I actively listen to others, valuing their perspectives and opinions.

I actively listen to others, valuing their perspectives and opinions. Actively listening to others is a critical component of showing respect. It involves giving others your full attention, asking questions to clarify their perspectives, and valuing their input and ideas. By actively listening, one can better understand the perspectives of others, foster open and honest communication, and build stronger relationships. Being transparent and honest in communication helps to foster trust and respect. By being approachable and willing to listen, you create an environment where open and honest communication is encouraged, leading to stronger relationships and improved collaboration.

Today's Leadership Affirmation:

I regularly conduct SWOT analysis to gain a comprehensive understanding of the organization's strengths, weaknesses, opportunities, and threats.

I regularly conduct SWOT analysis to gain a comprehensive understanding of the organization's strengths, weaknesses, opportunities, and threats. This affirmation highlights the importance of regularly conducting a SWOT analysis, which allows me to understand the internal and external factors that may impact the organization. This information is critical for making informed decisions and planning for the future. I will regularly conduct SWOT analysis to gain a comprehensive understanding of the environment. By conducting a thorough analysis of the internal and external factors that can impact the organization, I will be able to make informed decisions and develop effective strategies. This ongoing process of evaluation and planning will ensure that the organization remains competitive and well-positioned for success.

Today's Leadership Affirmation:

I understand the importance of transparency and actively work to keep my team members informed.

I understand the importance of transparency and actively work to keep my team members informed. Transparency is essential in any team or organization. By keeping my team members informed and up-to-date on important decisions and information, I foster trust and respect, and help to create a positive and productive work environment. I will prioritize transparency with my team members by proactively sharing important decisions and information with them. By keeping my team members informed, I will build trust and respect, and create an open and productive work environment where everyone feels valued and heard.

Today's Leadership Affirmation:

I stay informed of the latest technology trends and developments, and actively seek out ways to incorporate them into the organization.

I stay informed of the latest technology trends and developments, and actively seek out ways to incorporate them into the organization. In today's fast-paced business environment, technology is constantly evolving. I understand the importance of staying informed about the latest trends and developments in order to take advantage of the opportunities they offer. I actively seek out ways to incorporate new technology into the organization, knowing that this can help streamline operations, increase efficiency, and drive growth. As a dedicated professional, I understand that incorporating the latest technology into the organization is crucial to remain competitive in today's ever-changing business landscape. I make it a priority to stay informed. By doing so, I am able to ensure that the organization is utilizing the most advanced and efficient tools and systems available, ultimately resulting in improved performance and increased success.

Today's Leadership Affirmation:

I understand the importance of data security and privacy and take appropriate measures to protect the organization's and customers' information.

I understand the importance of data security and privacy and take appropriate measures to protect the organization's and customers' information. I understand that data security and privacy are of the utmost importance. I take appropriate measures to protect the organization's and customers' information. This includes implementing robust security protocols, conducting regular security audits and training my team members on best practices. I will prioritize the protection of the organization's and customers' information by taking appropriate measures. I understand that in today's digital landscape, data security and privacy are critical. To achieve this goal, today, I will implement robust security protocols to safeguard sensitive data, regularly conduct security audits to identify vulnerabilities, and proactively train my team members on best practices. I will stay informed of the latest security threats and work to update security measures as needed to stay ahead of potential risks.

Today's Leadership Affirmation:

I provide regular updates and progress reports to my team members, keeping them informed of the status of important projects and initiatives.

I provide regular updates and progress reports to my team members, keeping them informed of the status of important projects and initiatives. Regular communication is key to ensuring that team members are aware of the status of projects and initiatives, and keeping them informed helps build trust and respect. Providing updates helps to keep everyone on the same page and encourages active collaboration. I will prioritize being open and approachable to questions and feedback from my team members, recognizing that their concerns are valuable and important. Today, I will actively seek out feedback and address concerns in a timely and respectful manner, in order to build trust and respect within the team and foster a positive and productive work environment.

Today's Leadership Affirmation:

I am approachable and willing to listen, encouraging open and honest communication.

I am approachable and willing to listen, encouraging open and honest communication. Being approachable and willing to listen is an important aspect of showing respect to others. It involves being open and accessible to others, and actively encouraging open and honest communication. By being approachable and willing to listen, I will create an environment of trust and respect, where everyone feels comfortable sharing their ideas and opinions. By demonstrating these qualities, I will endeavor to earn the trust and respect of those around me, building strong and positive relationships that are essential for personal and professional success. Today, I will be available to my team and encourage them to share vital information with me. I will express openly how I value each exchange with my team members.

Today's Leadership Affirmation:

I am approachable and willing to listen, encouraging open and honest communication.

I am approachable and willing to listen, encouraging open and honest communication. Being approachable and willing to listen is an important aspect of showing respect to others. It involves being open and accessible to others, and actively encouraging open and honest communication. By being approachable and willing to listen, I will create an environment of trust and respect, where everyone feels comfortable sharing their ideas and opinions. By demonstrating these qualities, I will endeavor to earn the trust and respect of those around me, building strong and positive relationships that are essential for personal and professional success. Today, I will be available to my team and encourage them to share vital information with me. I will express openly how I value each exchange with my team members.

Today's Leadership Affirmation:

I am true to my values and beliefs, living them in my personal and professional life.

I am true to my values and beliefs, living them in my personal and professional life. I believe that it is important to live my values and beliefs, both in my personal and professional life. This helps me to be authentic and true to myself, which in turn helps me to lead by example and inspire my team members. I will continue to live my values and beliefs in my personal and professional life, and strive to be a consistent and authentic leader. I will make decisions and take actions that align with my principles, and hold myself accountable for upholding them. By living my values and being true to myself, I will inspire my team members to do the same and foster a culture of integrity within our organization.

Today's Leadership Affirmation:

I understand the importance of recruiting and retaining top talent, and actively seek out ways to attract and retain the best employees.

I understand the importance of recruiting and retaining top talent, and actively seek out ways to attract and retain the best employees. I will prioritize the recruitment and retention of top talent by actively seeking out ways to attract and retain the best employees. I recognize that the success of the organization depends on having a team of highly skilled and motivated individuals, and I will make this a priority. I will implement competitive compensation and benefits packages, create a positive and inclusive work environment, and provide opportunities for employee growth and development. By doing so, I will ensure that the organization is able to recruit and retain top talent, leading to continued success and growth. As a leader, I understand this importance. Today, I will actively seek out ways to attract and retain the best employees. I will use incentives such as competitive compensation and benefits

[34]

packages. I will create a positive and inclusive work environment, and provide opportunities for employee growth and development.

Today's Leadership Affirmation:

I use the results of SWOT analysis to inform strategic decision-making and planning.

I use the results of SWOT analysis to inform strategic decision-making and planning. The results of the SWOT analysis provide valuable insights that can inform decision making and planning. By understanding the organization's strengths, weaknesses, opportunities and threats, I can make more informed decisions that align with the organization's goals and objectives. This affirmation underscores the importance and my understanding of using the results of a SWOT analysis to inform strategic decision-making and planning. As a leader, I will use this approach to inform my decision making. By incorporating the insights gained from the analysis into decision-making processes, I can ensure that the organization is taking a comprehensive approach to planning and that we are making the most of our strengths and opportunities while addressing weaknesses and mitigating potential threats.

Today's Leadership Affirmation:

I am committed to maintaining open and transparent communication with my team members, keeping them informed and engaged.

I am committed to maintaining open and transparent communication with my team members, keeping them informed and engaged. Open and transparent communication is essential for building trust and fostering a sense of collaboration and teamwork, keeping everyone aligned toward the same goals. Through open lines of communication, I can more effectively manage the organization's daily operations. I will actively seek out opportunities to communicate with my team members and encourage them to share their ideas and feedback. I will provide my team with multiple avenues to engage me. Today, I will update them on important information, such as changes to the organization's policies, goals, and initiatives, to ensure that everyone is on the same page.

Today's Leadership Affirmation:

I foster a positive and inclusive work environment, valuing the diversity and unique perspectives of my team members.

I foster a positive and inclusive work environment, valuing the diversity and unique perspectives of my team members. A diverse and inclusive work environment not only promotes a sense of belonging but also brings a variety of perspectives and ideas to the table. I understand the importance of this and strive to create a work environment where every team member feels valued and respected. I will continue my ongoing effort and continuous commitment to foster a positive and inclusive work environment, valuing the diversity and unique perspectives of my team members for their unique contributions. I will ensure that every team member feels heard and respected, regardless of their background or identity. I understand that diversity and inclusion are essential to a thriving organization, and I am committed to promoting these values in all aspects of our work. Today, I will listen to and learn from my team members, creating a

[38]

safe space for open communication and collaboration. Together, we will work toward achieving our goals and driving the organization forward.

Today's Leadership Affirmation:

I provide opportunities for employee growth and development, both professionally and personally.

I provide opportunities for employee growth and development, both professionally and personally. I believe that providing opportunities for employee growth and development is essential for both the employee and the organization. As a leader, I actively seek out opportunities for my team members to develop, both professionally and personally. This may include providing training and developmental programs, mentoring, and other opportunities for professional growth. I recognize that investing in the growth and development of my team members is an investment in the future of the organization. I understand that when employees are given the opportunity to grow, they are more engaged, motivated, and committed to the success of the organization. As a leader, I will actively seek out opportunities for my team members to learn and develop new skills, whether it be through training programs, mentoring, or other avenues for personal and professional growth.

Today's Leadership Affirmation:

I understand the importance of work-life balance and actively seek out ways to promote it among my team members.

As a leader, I recognize that work-life balance is crucial for employee satisfaction and overall well-being, and I am dedicated to promoting it among my team members. Work-life balance is important for employee well-being and job satisfaction. Practices to achieve balance among my team members may include providing flexible scheduling options, encouraging time off, and promoting overall well-being. I recognize the importance of creating a culture that values mental health and wellness, and I am dedicated to providing resources and support to ensure that my team members feel empowered to prioritize their own well-being. By prioritizing their well-being, I am confident that my team members will be happier, healthier, and more productive, ultimately leading to the success of our organization. I will promote the importance of work-life balance and implement strategies that encourage this balance. Today, I will offer flexible scheduling options, encouraging regular breaks and time off, and providing resources and support for my team members to prioritize their well-being.

Today's Leadership Affirmation:

I understand the potential impact of change on my team members and take appropriate measures to minimize disruption and ensure a smooth transition.

I understand the potential impact of change on my team members and take appropriate measures to minimize disruption and ensure a smooth transition. I am aware that change can be disruptive and difficult for team members. I take appropriate measures to minimize disruption and ensure a smooth transition, such as providing training and support. I understand that change can have a significant impact on my team members and may cause disruption. To minimize the impact, I take appropriate measures and provide necessary support to ensure a smooth transition. This includes providing adequate training, clear communication, and addressing any concerns or questions that may arise. I am committed to making the change process as seamless as possible for my team members. Today, I will assess the resources we need to assist us in managing change.

Today's Leadership Affirmation:

I actively encourage my team members to disconnect after work hours.

I actively encourage my team members to disconnect after work hours. This means not expecting them to be constantly available outside of work and promoting activities that help them rest and build resilience. I understand the importance of disconnecting after work hours and encourage my team members to do so. I will proactively monitor available overtime activities and ensure employees are allocating personal time. I encourage my team members to prioritize their well-being and not feel obligated to be constantly available or on-call. I will ensure I pay employees for their time worked. By adopting these practices, I can help reduce their stress levels and improve their overall well-being. Today, I will make sure my team understands my expectations and emphasize well-being as a priority.

Today's Leadership Affirmation:

I am sensitive to the diverse needs of my team members and work to create a flexible and inclusive work environment.

I am sensitive to the diverse needs of my team members and work to create a flexible and inclusive work environment. As a manager, I understand the importance of creating a work environment that is inclusive and accommodating to the diverse needs of all my team members. I make it a priority to be aware of and address any potential barriers that may exist for certain team members and actively work to create a more equitable and inclusive space for everyone to thrive in. I will continue to prioritize creating a flexible and inclusive work environment that is sensitive to the diverse needs of my team members. I will actively listen and be aware of the unique needs and perspectives of each team member, and work to create a space where everyone feels valued and respected. I will address any potential barriers and take action to create a more equitable and inclusive workplace for my team.

Today's Leadership Affirmation:

I support my team members in setting boundaries and managing work-life balance.

I support my team members in setting boundaries and managing work-life balance. I understand that maintaining a healthy balance between work and personal life is essential for the health of my team members. I am committed to helping them set realistic boundaries and manage their workloads in a way that allows them to achieve a balance. This may involve providing coaching and support, or helping to identify and eliminate sources of stress. I recognize the importance of achieving a healthy balance between work and personal life, and I am willing to provide guidance, coaching, and support to help my team members achieve this. I am committed to supporting my team members and I will actively listen to their concerns and needs, and work collaboratively with them to identify strategies that work for them.

[48]

Today's Leadership Affirmation:

I lead by example and maintain a healthy work-life balance myself.

I lead by example and maintain a healthy work-life balance myself. I believe that leading by example is important, and I strive to maintain a balance between my work and personal life as well, so my team members can see that it is possible. I prioritize my own work-life balance. I understand that maintaining a healthy balance between work and personal life is essential for both my well-being and productivity, and I strive to model this for my team members. I also prioritize self-care and make time for activities that bring me joy and relaxation outside of work. This not only helps me to be a more effective leader, but also sets an example for my team members and encourages them to prioritize their own well-being.

Today's Leadership Affirmation:

I provide opportunities for remote and flexible working arrangements, when possible, to help my team members achieve a better balance.

I provide opportunities for remote and flexible working arrangements, when possible, to help my team members achieve a better balance. I understand that remote and flexible working arrangements can be beneficial for work-life balance, and I make sure to provide these opportunities when possible. I recognize that these arrangements can be beneficial for improving well-being, reducing stress, and increasing productivity. As a leader, I am committed to ensuring that my team members have the necessary resources and support to work remotely and flexibly, including access to technology and communication tools. I practice being flexible and adaptable in the workplace to accommodate the needs of team members and promote a healthy work-life balance. Today, I will help my team members achieve a better balance between their work and personal lives.

[50]

Today's Leadership Affirmation:

I understand the importance of regular breaks and downtime, and encourage my team members to take them.

I understand the importance of regular breaks and downtime, and encourage my team members to take them. I highlight with my junior leaders the importance of encouraging our team members to take regular breaks to avoid burnout and to promote well-being. Encouraging team members to take regular breaks and downtime is crucial for their physical and mental health, and it helps them to maintain a healthy work-life balance. By acknowledging the importance of breaks and actively promoting them, I can create a more positive and supportive work environment. Ultimately, being aware of the pace of work and encouraging team members to take regular breaks and downtime prevents burnout and promotes well-being, which in turn can lead to increased productivity and job satisfaction.

Today's Leadership Affirmation:

*I believe in the power of diversity and different
perspectives when solving problems, and actively seek out
the input and ideas of others.*

I believe in the power of diversity and different
perspectives when solving problems, and actively seek out
the input and ideas of others. I know that by valuing
different perspectives, I can find more innovative and
effective solutions. I actively seek out the input and ideas
of others. By valuing the unique perspectives and
experiences of my team members, I can foster a
collaborative environment that encourages creative
problem solving and the development of new ideas. I
recognize that everyone brings something unique to the
table, and by embracing diversity and inclusion in the
problem-solving process, I can ensure that the best
solutions are identified and implemented.

Today's Leadership Affirmation:

I actively communicate with my team members, keeping them informed and engaged.

I actively communicate with my team members, keeping them informed and engaged. Communication is key to employee engagement, and by actively communicating with my team members, I keep them informed and engaged in the organization's goals and objectives. This helps to create a sense of shared purpose and ownership among my team members, and fosters a culture of open and transparent communication. I understand the importance of active communication with my team members and prioritize keeping them informed and engaged in the organization's goals and objectives. By fostering a culture of open and transparent communication, I help create a sense of shared purpose and ownership among my team members, promoting their engagement and contributing to the organization's success.

Today's Leadership Affirmation:

I actively seek out feedback on work-life balance and make adjustments as needed to support my team members.

I actively seek out feedback on work-life balance and make adjustments as needed to support my team members. I understand that work-life balance is an ongoing process and therefore I actively seek out feedback from my team members about how I can support them better. This allows me to make adjustments and improvements as needed to ensure that my team members are able to achieve a healthy balance. I actively seek feedback from my team members on their work-life balance and am committed to making adjustments as needed to support them. I understand that achieving a healthy work-life balance is an ongoing process, and I strive to create an environment where my team members feel comfortable sharing their feedback. By regularly seeking and acting on feedback, I can ensure that my team members feel supported and empowered to achieve a healthy balance.

Today's Leadership Affirmation:

I understand the importance of mentoring and coaching, and actively seek out ways to provide it to my team members.

I understand the importance of mentoring and coaching, and actively seek out ways to provide it to my team members. Mentoring and coaching are critical to the growth and development of team members, and as a leader, it is important to recognize this and actively seek out ways to provide it. This can include setting up regular mentoring sessions, providing guidance and support when needed, and being a role model for the team. As a leader, I proactively seek out opportunities to provide guidance, support, and feedback to help them achieve their personal and professional goals. By investing in their growth, I empower them to become their best selves and contribute to the success of the team and the organization. I value mentoring and coaching as powerful tools for fostering my own growth and development and I will extend this to my team members.

Today's Leadership Affirmation:

I am a proactive leader.

I am a proactive leader. As such, I understand that my actions have a direct impact on the success of my team and organization. I recognize the importance of being proactive in my decision-making process to stay ahead of the curve and achieve our strategic goals. I understand that a successful strategic vision requires taking action and making strategic decisions in a timely manner I will prioritize those that align with our strategic vision and have the greatest potential to generate value for our organization. I will also evaluate the risks and challenges associated with each initiative and develop contingency plans to mitigate them. Today, I will review our current initiatives and make decisions about which projects to prioritize and which to deprioritize. I will take the necessary steps to move our organization forward and make progress toward our objectives, staying proactive and nimble to adapt to changing circumstances.

Today's Leadership Affirmation:

I provide guidance and support to my team members to help them achieve their goals.

I provide guidance and support to my team members to help them achieve their goals. One of my key roles as a leader is to support my team members in achieving their goals. I do this by providing guidance and support, whether it be through offering advice, connecting them with resources, or providing the necessary training. I am committed to helping my team members succeed. As a leader, I recognize that it is essential to support my team members in achieving, both professional and personal goals. To do this, I will actively listen to their aspirations and provide them with tailored feedback and support. This may include offering mentorship, providing resources or training, or connecting them with relevant networks. I am committed to helping my team members achieve their goals and will work tirelessly to ensure their success. Today, I will provide relevant guidance to my team members to help them achieve their professional goals.

Today's Leadership Affirmation:

I provide opportunities for my team members to take on leadership roles and responsibilities.

I provide opportunities for my team members to take on leadership roles and responsibilities. As a leader, it is important to provide opportunities for team members to take on leadership roles and responsibilities. This can include delegating tasks and projects, as well as providing mentoring and coaching to help them develop the necessary skills and knowledge. Additionally, I understand that providing these opportunities can also help to increase team members' engagement and motivation, as they feel valued and trusted by their leader. I am committed to creating a supportive environment that encourages team members to take on new challenges and grow as leaders, while also providing them with the necessary support and guidance to succeed.

Today's Leadership Affirmation:

I am approachable and available to my team members, providing guidance and support as needed.

I am approachable and available to my team members, providing guidance and support as needed. A leader should be approachable and available to team members, providing guidance and support as needed. This can include being available for questions, providing feedback and coaching, and being a sounding board for ideas and concerns. I will make a conscious effort to be approachable and available to my team members, actively seeking out opportunities to provide guidance and support when needed. I understand that being present and supportive is key to building trust and respect within a team, and I am committed to fostering an open and supportive environment where my team members feel comfortable coming to me with any questions or concerns.

Today's Leadership Affirmation:

I am transparent and honest in my feedback, helping my team members identify their strengths and weaknesses.

I am transparent and honest in my feedback, helping my team members identify their strengths and weaknesses. I believe that providing transparent and honest feedback is essential for the growth and development of my team. I make a point to provide clear and actionable feedback that helps my team members identify their strengths and weaknesses. I believe that by providing transparent and honest feedback, I am helping my team members to improve and grow. Thus, today, I will provide transparent and honest feedback to my team members, helping them identify their strengths and areas for improvement. By doing so, I will create a culture of growth and development within my team, and empower my team members to continuously improve and excel.

Today's Leadership Affirmation:

I actively seek out opportunities for professional development and provide them to my team members.

I actively seek out opportunities for professional development and provide them to my team members. I understand that to be successful, everyone needs to continue learning and developing their skills. I am committed to providing opportunities for professional development to my team members, so that they can achieve their full potential. As a leader, I recognize the importance of continuous learning and professional development for myself and my team members. I actively seek out opportunities for professional development and encourage my team members to do the same. I believe that investing in our skills and knowledge not only helps us to be more effective in our roles but also contributes to our personal growth and career advancement. Therefore, I will make it a priority to provide resources, training, and support to my team members to help them achieve their professional-development goals.

Today's Leadership Affirmation:

I actively listen to my team members, providing constructive feedback and coaching to help them improve.

I actively listen to my team members, providing constructive feedback and coaching to help them improve. Listening is a key aspect of being an effective leader, and it is important to actively listen to team members to understand their needs and concerns. This can include providing constructive feedback and coaching to help them improve, and being open to their ideas and suggestions. As a leader, I understand the importance of actively listening. By listening to their needs and concerns, I can provide constructive feedback and coaching to help them improve. I am committed to creating a supportive and collaborative environment where my team members feel comfortable sharing their ideas and suggestions. Through active listening and open communication, I strive to help my team members achieve their goals and reach their full potential.

Today's Leadership Affirmation:

I understand the importance of leadership presence and actively work to cultivate it.

I understand the importance of leadership presence and actively work to cultivate it. Leadership presence is the ability to project confidence, authority, and authenticity, and it is an important aspect of being an effective leader. A leader should understand the importance of leadership presence and actively work to cultivate it, by being aware of their body language, nonverbal communication, and personal brand. Building and maintaining a strong leadership presence is crucial for establishing credibility, inspiring confidence, and fostering trust among team members. A leader who exudes confidence and authority is more likely to be perceived as credible, and can better influence and motivate their team. Additionally, cultivating an authentic personal brand can help a leader connect with their team members on a more personal level, further strengthening their leadership presence.

Today's Leadership Affirmation:

I am confident and assertive in my communication and actions, inspiring trust and respect among my team members.

I am confident and assertive in my communication and actions, inspiring trust and respect among my team members. Confidence and assertiveness in communication and actions are key traits of a strong leader. I understand that my team members look to me for guidance and direction, and I ensure that my communication and actions are clear, decisive and confident. This inspires trust and respect among my team members and they are more likely to follow my lead. I will continue to develop my confidence and assertiveness in communication and actions, as I recognize that it is crucial to inspire trust and respect among my team members. To do so, I will actively seek feedback and coaching to improve my communication skills, practice decision-making, and assertiveness in a variety of situations. I will also take the time to reflect on my values and how they influence my leadership style, ensuring that I am authentic and true to myself while leading by example.

Today's Leadership Affirmation:

I am authentic and true to myself, leading by example and living my values.

I am authentic and true to myself, leading by example and living my values. Being authentic and true to oneself is essential for effective leadership. I believe my actions help to inspire trust and respect among my team members. I believe that by being true to myself, I am better able to connect with my team members and understand their needs and concerns. I prioritize being authentic as a leader. By doing so, I am able to create a positive work environment and inspire trust and respect among my team members. I believe that being authentic also helps me to be more empathetic and understanding toward my team members, which allows me to better support them in their roles.

Today's Leadership Affirmation:

I am aware of my body language and nonverbal communication, using it to project confidence and authority.

I am aware of my body language and nonverbal communication, using it to project confidence and authority. As a leader, it is important to be aware of one's body language and nonverbal communication as it can greatly impact how one is perceived by others. This helps to inspire trust and respect among my team members and can greatly enhance the effectiveness of my communication. As a leader, I understand that my nonverbal communication can greatly impact how I am perceived by others. Therefore, I will actively watch my nonverbal communication, and use it effectively. By doing so, I believe I can inspire trust and respect among my team members, and greatly enhance the effectiveness of my communication. Today, I will be aware of my body language and nonverbal communication, using it to project confidence and authority.

Today's Leadership Affirmation:

I am able to think critically and make decisions quickly, demonstrating my ability to lead under pressure.

I am able to think critically and make decisions quickly, demonstrating my ability to lead under pressure. As a leader, being able to think critically and make quick, well-informed decisions is essential. I understand that in high-pressure situations, my team members will look to me for guidance and direction. I am able to stay calm and level-headed, and make decisions that are in the best interest of my team and our goals. I am confident in my ability to think critically and make quick, well-informed decisions under pressure. As a leader, I understand that my team members look to me for guidance and I will stay calm and level-headed, and make decisions that are in the best interest of my team and our goals.

Today's Leadership Affirmation:

I am able to effectively communicate and articulate my vision, inspiring others to follow.

I am able to effectively communicate and articulate my vision, inspiring others to follow. Effective communication is a key aspect of leadership. I am able to effectively communicate my vision and inspire others to follow by being clear and concise, and by effectively articulating my ideas and goals. This helps my team members understand what we are working toward and how they can contribute to the success of the team. I will continue to develop my communication skills to effectively articulate my vision and goals, inspiring and motivating my team members to work toward a common goal. I will strive to be clear and concise in my communication, so that my team members understand the direction we are heading in and feel motivated to contribute to our success.

Today's Leadership Affirmation:

I am able to inspire and motivate my team members, leading them toward a common goal.

I am able to inspire and motivate my team members, leading them toward a common goal. Inspiration and motivation are essential for a team to be successful. I am able to inspire and motivate my team members by setting clear goals, providing regular feedback, and recognizing their achievements. By leading my team toward a common goal, I am able to help them work together effectively and achieve great results. I am committed to my team members, leading them toward a common goal with increased energy and purpose. I will regularly provide clear goals, feedback, and recognition for their achievements. By setting an example and fostering a positive team environment, I will encourage my team members to work together effectively and achieve their full potential.

Today's Leadership Affirmation:

I am approachable and open to feedback, fostering trust and respect among my team members.

I am approachable and open to feedback, fostering trust and respect among my team members. I understand the importance of fostering a positive and open team culture. I am available to my team members, and actively seek out feedback on my leadership in an attempt to understand how I can improve. I respect my team members opinions and make adjustments as needed to earn their trust and support their growth and development. I will continue to prioritize being approachable and open to feedback from my team members. I will actively seek out opportunities for feedback and be open and receptive to any constructive criticism or suggestions for improvement. By fostering a culture of trust and respect, I can build stronger relationships with my team members and create a more positive work environment. Today, I will listen to others and adjust my approach according to their needs. I will encourage all leaders to build trust with their teams.

[71]

Today's Leadership Affirmation:

I am able to command a room and command attention, when necessary, to effectively lead and communicate.

I am able to command a room and command attention, when necessary, to effectively lead and communicate. This affirmation highlights the importance of being able to command attention and effectively communicate in high-stakes situations. A leader who can do this is better equipped to lead and communicate effectively in important meetings, presentations, and other critical moments. I am able to command a room and command attention when necessary. As a leader, I understand the importance of being able to communicate effectively and command attention in high-stakes situations. I am confident and articulate, and able to convey my message clearly and effectively, even in challenging circumstances. I am able to inspire and motivate others, and lead my team toward success.

Today's Leadership Affirmation:

I am able to adapt my leadership style and approach as needed, to effectively lead and inspire my team.

I am able to adapt my leadership style and approach as needed, to effectively lead and inspire my team. A good leader must be able to adapt their leadership style and approach to fit the needs of their team. This allows me to be effective in different situations and to get the best out of my team members, regardless of the specific challenges we may be facing. I am able to assess a situation and determine the best approach to achieve our goals. This approach allows me to be effective in different situations and to get the best out of my team members, regardless of the specific challenges we may be facing. Today, I will reflect on what style is best to apply to a certain situation. I will be open to understanding more about the concept of situational leadership and I will apply myself to my team's needs to effectively lead and inspire them.

Today's Leadership Affirmation:

I understand the importance of authenticity and actively work to be true to myself.

Authenticity is a crucial aspect of personal and professional growth and is key to establishing trust and respect among team members. As a leader, I understand the importance of being true to myself and actively work to embody this principle in my communication and actions. I will continue to prioritize authenticity in my personal and professional life. I will regularly reflect on my values and beliefs to ensure that my actions and communication align with them. I will be transparent and honest with my team members and strive to create a culture of openness and trust. By being true to myself, I will lead with integrity and inspire my team to do the same.

Today's Leadership Affirmation:

I am honest and transparent in my communication and actions.

I am honest and transparent in my communication and actions. Honesty and transparency are essential to building trust and respect among my team members. I believe that being open and genuine with my team members helps to foster a positive and productive work environment. I will continue to prioritize honesty and transparency in all my communication and actions as a leader. I will make a conscious effort to share information and provide feedback openly and honestly, even when it may be difficult. By doing so, I will continue to build trust and respect among my team, ultimately leading to greater success and productivity.

Today's Leadership Affirmation:

I am proactive in identifying and addressing potential issues with technology solutions, ensuring continuity of operations.

I am proactive in identifying and addressing potential issues with technology solutions, ensuring continuity of operations. I understand that technology solutions, like any other system, can sometimes experience issues. I am proactive in identifying and addressing potential issues, ensuring continuity of operations. By being proactive, I can prevent small issues from becoming big problems and ensure that the organization can continue to operate smoothly. I will remain proactive in identifying and addressing potential issues with technology solutions, to ensure continuity of operations for our organization. I understand that technology is a critical component of our operations and that any issues with these systems can significantly impact our ability to function effectively. To achieve this, today, I will take a proactive approach to monitoring and maintaining our technology solutions. I will regularly review our systems and identify potential issues before they become major problems. I will also work closely with our IT team to ensure that they have the necessary resources to address any issues that arise quickly.

Today's Leadership Affirmation:

I am committed to building a strong financial foundation, ensuring the long-term sustainability of the organization.

I am fully committed to building a strong financial foundation for our organization, and I will do everything in my power to ensure our long-term sustainability and success. This commitment will ensure the long-term sustainability and success of our organization. With an unwavering focus on fiscal responsibility, I will consistently seek out opportunities to maximize profitability, minimize risk, and create sustainable growth. I will take a proactive approach to financial management, constantly analyzing our financial performance and seeking out innovative ways to optimize our financial strategy. Through sound financial planning, disciplined execution, and a steadfast dedication to our long-term goals, I am confident that we will achieve sustained success and growth for many years to come.

Today's Leadership Affirmation:

I am self-aware and actively work to understand and improve myself.

I am self-aware and actively work to understand and improve myself. I believe that self-awareness is essential to being a leader. I actively work to understand and improve myself; this helps me to be a better leader and a better person. I will commit to cultivating self-awareness and continuously improving myself as a leader. By consistently reflecting on my actions, thoughts, and emotions, I will gain a better understanding of my strengths and weaknesses. This awareness will allow me to identify areas where I can improve and develop new skills. Through this process, I will become a more effective leader and inspire my team members to do the same.

Today's Leadership Affirmation:

I am open to feedback and willing to make changes to improve myself.

I am open to feedback and willing to make changes to improve myself. I believe that being open to feedback is essential to being a leader. I am willing to make changes to improve myself and my leadership skills. I will actively seek out feedback from my team members and other stakeholders, and be open to constructive criticism. By doing so, I can gain valuable insights into my strengths and areas for improvement, and use that feedback to continuously develop myself as a leader. I will also take action on that feedback, making changes where necessary and following up with my team members to ensure that their feedback has been heard and addressed. I will encourage my team members to share their thoughts and ideas by providing a safe and supportive space for them to do so. This will involve actively seeking out and creating opportunities for brainstorming and collaboration, as well as being receptive to feedback from team members during meetings and one-on-one interactions. This process will not only help me to become a better leader, but also create a culture of open communication and growth within my team.

Today's Leadership Affirmation:

I am confident in who I am, and am not afraid to be my true self in any situation.

I am confident in who I am, and am not afraid to be my true self in any situation. I believe that confidence is essential to being a leader. I will continue to cultivate my confidence and authenticity, embracing my unique qualities and experiences as strengths. By being true to myself and demonstrating confidence, I can inspire my team members to do the same. I will lead by example, encouraging my team members to be confident in their own abilities and to bring their unique perspectives to the table. This will create a culture of acceptance and inclusivity, where everyone feels empowered to contribute and succeed. Today, I will remind myself to embrace confidence in who I am, and be my true self in all situations.

Today's Leadership Affirmation:

I foster an environment of open communication and collaboration within the team when making decisions.

I foster an environment of open communication and collaboration within the team when making decisions. I believe that open communication and collaboration lead to better decisions. By fostering a culture of open communication, I ensure that all team members feel heard and valued. I will foster an environment of open communication and collaboration within the team when making decisions. I will actively encourage all team members to share their thoughts and ideas, and ensure that everyone feels heard and valued. By fostering a culture of open communication, I will help create a more inclusive and effective decision-making process, ultimately leading to better decisions for the team. Today, I will solicit input on our initiatives from team members and stakeholders ensuring all have a seat at the table.

Today's Leadership Affirmation:

I treat others with dignity and fairness, regardless of their position or background.

I treat others with dignity and fairness, regardless of their position or background. Treating others with dignity and fairness is an essential aspect of showing respect. It means being respectful, non-judgmental, and impartial in your interactions with others. This helps create a positive work environment where everyone feels valued and respected, regardless of their position or background. Fostering a positive and inclusive work environment is essential in valuing the diversity and unique perspectives of others. This approach requires awareness and sensitivity to cultural and individual differences, and treating everyone with respect. Today, I will understand how I engage with others, consciously ensure I extend respect, and assist others to maintain their dignity in all my interactions.

Today's Leadership Affirmation:

I understand the importance of respect in building and maintaining strong relationships, both personally and professionally.

I understand the importance of respect in building and maintaining strong relationships, both personally and professionally. Respect is a fundamental aspect of all successful relationships, and this affirmation highlights the importance of cultivating respect in both personal and professional contexts. By treating others with dignity and fairness, and valuing their perspectives and opinions, it is possible to build strong and enduring relationships based on mutual respect. I will work to actively cultivate respect, recognizing that it is a foundational element of growing and sustaining strong connections with others. By treating my team members with dignity, fairness, and valuing their perspectives and opinions, I will strive to create an environment of mutual respect that fosters positive and enduring relationships.

Today's Leadership Affirmation:

I recognize the importance of work-life balance and consider it when making decisions about workloads and schedules.

I recognize the importance of work-life balance and consider it when making decisions about workloads and schedules. I understand that maintaining a healthy balance between work and personal life is essential for the well-being of my team members. I am committed to considering work-life balance when making decisions about workloads, schedules, and other factors that may impact my team. I look for ways to assist my team in reducing stress. I promote a positive work environment, such as providing opportunities for my team members to disconnect and recharge, encouraging them to prioritize their well-being, and providing resources and support to help them achieve a healthy balance. By providing resources and support and creating a positive work environment, you can help your team members achieve a healthy balance between work and personal life, leading to

[86]

increased engagement, productivity, and overall satisfaction.

Today's Leadership Affirmation:

I am aware of and sensitive to the cultural and individual differences of others, treating them with respect.

I am aware of and sensitive to the cultural and individual differences of others, treating them with respect. I believe that a diverse and inclusive work environment is essential to creating a positive and productive workplace culture. Understanding and being sensitive to the cultural and individual differences of others is an important aspect of showing respect. I do this by recognizing and valuing the unique perspectives and experiences of others, and treating them with respect, even if they are different from my own perspectives and I will strive to value and appreciate these differences. Today, I will make a conscious effort to avoid assumptions and stereotypes, and treat each team member with the respect they deserve, regardless of their background or identity. By being aware and sensitive to the cultural and individual differences of others, I will create a more positive and inclusive work environment.

Today's Leadership Affirmation:

I involve my team members in the decision-making process, valuing their input and perspectives.

I involve my team members in the decision-making process, valuing their input and perspectives. By involving team members in the decision-making process, leaders show their respect for the opinions and expertise of their team. This not only fosters a positive work environment, but can also lead to better decision-making and improved outcomes. I will prioritize involving my team; by actively seeking out the opinions and expertise of my team members, I can demonstrate that their contributions are valued and that their perspectives are essential to our success. This approach can lead to better decisions and a more collaborative work environment, where everyone feels supported and heard.

Today's Leadership Affirmation:

I am committed to maintaining open and transparent communication with my team members, respecting their needs and concerns.

I am committed to maintaining open and transparent communication with my team members, respecting their needs and concerns. By maintaining open and transparent communication, I aim to build trust and respect with my team members. By respecting their needs and concerns, I show that their thoughts and opinions are valued, which can create a positive and productive work environment. I will actively work to maintain open and transparent communication with my team members, by regularly checking in with them and addressing their concerns promptly. I recognize that effective communication is essential for building trust and respect, which can lead to a more positive and productive work environment. I will respect my team members' needs and concerns by creating a safe and supportive space for them to share their thoughts and opinions. By actively listening to their feedback and ideas, I can foster a culture of open communication and mutual respect.

Today's Leadership Affirmation:

I actively communicate with my team members, keeping them informed of important decisions and their reasoning.

I actively communicate with my team members, keeping them informed of important decisions and their reasoning. Open and consistent communication is key to ensuring that everyone is on the same page and working toward the same goals. By keeping my team members informed and providing context for my decisions, I help to build trust and create a collaborative work environment. I will prioritize open and consistent communication with my team members, keeping them informed of important decisions and the reasoning behind them. By proactively sharing information and providing context, I will foster a sense of trust and collaboration among the team, and help to create a more positive and productive work environment.

Today's Leadership Affirmation:

I implement cost-saving measures, such as energy-efficient technologies and streamlined processes.

I implement cost-saving measures, such as energy-efficient technologies and streamlined processes. In addition to identifying cost-saving opportunities, I also take action to implement measures that will actually reduce expenses. By implementing energy-efficient technologies and streamlining processes, I am able to decrease costs while also improving efficiency. I will actively implement cost-saving measures to reduce expenses and improve the efficiency of the organization's operations. I recognize the importance of taking action and making tangible changes to achieve cost savings. By streamlining processes and eliminating waste, I will also increase efficiency and productivity within the organization. Through my efforts, I will help the organization achieve its financial goals while also creating a more sustainable future for the organization.

Today's Leadership Affirmation:

I understand the importance of trust, and actively work to earn it by being transparent and honest with my team members.

I understand the importance of trust, and actively work to earn it by being transparent and honest with my team members. Trust is a crucial component of any healthy relationship, and it is especially important in the workplace. Leaders who are transparent and honest with their team members help to build trust and create a positive work environment where everyone feels valued and respected. I will actively work to earn the trust of my team members by being transparent and honest with them. I understand the importance of building and maintaining trust in the workplace, and I will prioritize open communication, honesty, and transparency with my team. By doing so, I will foster a positive work environment where team members feel comfortable sharing their ideas and concerns, and where we can work collaboratively toward our goals. I am committed to earning and maintaining the trust of my team members, and to creating a workplace culture built on mutual respect and transparency.

Today's Leadership Affirmation:

I am sensitive to the diverse needs and backgrounds of my team members, creating an inclusive work environment.

I am sensitive to the diverse needs and backgrounds of my team members, creating an inclusive work environment. This affirmation emphasizes the importance of being sensitive to the diverse needs and backgrounds of team members, celebrating them and fostering inclusivity and harmony. By being sensitive to these needs, I can ensure that all my team members feel valued and respected. I recognize that everyone brings unique perspectives and experiences to the team, and I will make a conscious effort to create an environment that celebrates diversity and promotes inclusivity. Today, I will actively seek out opportunities to listen and learn about my team members. I will engage in open and empathetic conversations to better understand their unique perspectives and experiences. Through my actions and leadership, I will create an inclusive work environment where everyone feels valued and respected.

Today's Leadership Affirmation:

I am open to feedback and willing to make adjustments as needed, based on the input of others.

I am open to feedback and willing to make adjustments as needed, based on the input of others. Being open to feedback is crucial in continuously improving oneself. By being willing to receive and act on feedback, I can demonstrate a commitment to growth and a willingness to learn from others. This helps to build trust and respect, both personally and professionally. I will actively seek out feedback and be open to making adjustments based on the input of others. By being receptive to feedback and taking action on it, I will demonstrate my commitment to personal and professional growth. This will help me to build stronger relationships with others and foster an environment of open communication and collaboration. Today, I will be receptive to feedback, I will improve myself and my work, and build stronger relationships based on mutual respect and trust.

Today's Leadership Affirmation:

I am able to follow and implement the strategies and decisions of leadership, while also providing constructive feedback.

I am able to follow and implement the strategies and decisions of leadership, while also providing constructive feedback. As a team player, I understand the importance of following the lead of my superiors. However, I am not afraid to share my insights and thoughts when necessary. I believe that constructive feedback can help improve decisions and contribute to the success of the organization. I will provide feedback in a respectful and constructive manner, with the aim of improving decisions and helping the organization achieve its goals. By doing so, I can contribute to the success of the organization and help create a culture of open communication and collaboration. Today, I will strive to communicate my feedback in a respectful and productive manner, always with the goal of improving the overall performance and success of the organization.

Today's Leadership Affirmation:

I understand the importance of being a team player and actively work to improve my skills in this area.

I understand the importance of being a team player and actively work to improve my skills in this area. I understand the importance of teamwork in achieving success and I am committed to being a team player. I actively work to improve my skills in this area, making sure that I am always putting the team's goals first. I will continue to prioritize being a team player and actively work to improve my skills in this area. I understand that effective teamwork is crucial for achieving success, and I am committed to contributing to the success of the team. This means consistently putting the team's goals first, and actively seeking opportunities to collaborate and support my colleagues. I will continue to improve my communication, collaboration, and adaptability skills, so that I can effectively work with others toward a common goal.

Today's Leadership Affirmation:

I am a leader who is able to provide my team members with the necessary support and recognition for their work.

I am a leader who is able to provide my team members with the necessary support and recognition for their work. Providing support and recognition to team members is important in building and maintaining a motivated and productive team. As a leader, I make it a priority to ensure that my team members feel valued and supported in their work. I am committed to being a leader who provides my team members with appropriate recognition for their work. I understand that acknowledging their contributions and offering support can go a long way in motivating and retaining talented individuals. I strive to provide regular feedback, offer opportunities for professional development, and celebrate their achievements, fostering a positive and productive work environment.

Today's Leadership Affirmation:

I am a leader who is able to create a culture of continuous improvement and support for my team.

I am a leader who is able to create a culture of continuous improvement and support for my team. A culture of continuous improvement and support is essential for success. As a leader, I work to create an environment that encourages and supports my team members in their growth and development, both personally and professionally. I am committed to creating a culture of continuous improvement and support for my team. I understand the importance of fostering an environment that encourages learning and growth, and I make it a priority to provide my team members with opportunities for professional development. Today, I will encourage experimentation and risk-taking, and remain open to feedback, ensuring that my team feels supported in their growth both personally and professionally.

Today's Leadership Affirmation:

I am a leader who is able to understand the impact of my own emotions on my team and organization and regulate them accordingly.

I am a leader who is able to understand the impact of my own emotions on my team and organization and regulate them accordingly. By understanding the impact of my own emotions, I am able to regulate them in a way that benefits both my team and the organization as a whole. This helps me to maintain a professional demeanor, even in stressful or challenging situations, and to communicate effectively with my team and other stakeholders. As a leader, it's important to be aware of the impact of my emotions on others. I will regulate my emotions in a way that promotes a positive environment. This approach will help create a more productive and effective team, as well as build stronger relationships with stakeholders.

[102]

Today's Leadership Affirmation:

I understand the importance of employee engagement and actively seek out ways to increase it.

I understand the importance of employee engagement and actively seek out ways to increase it. Employee engagement is crucial to the success of any organization and I am committed to identifying and implementing strategies to keep my team members motivated and invested in their work. I understand the critical role that employee engagement plays in the success of an organization, and I am committed to actively seeking out ways to increase it. I believe that engaged team members are more motivated, productive, and committed to the success of the organization. To promote employee engagement, I regularly communicate with my team members, listen to their feedback, and provide opportunities for professional development and growth.

Today's Leadership Affirmation:

I foster a culture of fiscal responsibility within the organization, encouraging all employees to be mindful of financial resources.

I firmly believe in fostering a culture of fiscal responsibility within our organization. As a leader, it is my responsibility to ensure that all employees are aware of the value of financial resources and to encourage them to take an active role in managing these resources effectively. To this end, I am committed to providing regular training and education on financial best practices, and I will lead by example in demonstrating responsible financial decision-making. I will encourage all employees to be mindful of how they use financial resources and to look for opportunities to optimize spending, reduce waste, and increase efficiency. I understand that building a culture of fiscal responsibility is critical to our long-term success, and I will work tirelessly to ensure that this mindset is ingrained in every aspect of our organization. By fostering a culture of fiscal responsibility, we will create a more efficient, cost-effective, and sustainable organization. We will be better positioned to invest in growth and innovation, to weather economic downturns, and to achieve our long-term strategic goals. Today, I affirm that I am fully committed to fostering a culture of fiscal responsibility within our organization, and I will do everything in my power to encourage all employees to be mindful of financial resources and to take an active role in financial management.

Today's Leadership Affirmation:

I am willing to be flexible with working hours when necessary to accommodate my team members' personal commitments.

I am willing to be flexible with working hours when necessary to accommodate my team members' personal commitments. I understand that my team members have personal commitments outside of work and am willing to be flexible with working hours when necessary to accommodate them. This includes being open to flexible scheduling and remote work arrangements. I will prioritize the well-being of my team members by being willing to be flexible with working hours when necessary to accommodate their personal commitments. This means actively listening to their needs and being open to considering flexible scheduling options or remote work arrangements to ensure they can balance their personal and professional obligations effectively.

Today's Leadership Affirmation:

I provide a healthy and comfortable working environment to promote well-being and balance.

I provide a healthy and comfortable working environment to promote well-being and balance. By creating a healthy and comfortable working environment, I promote the well-being and balance of my team members. This may include things like providing comfortable seating, natural lighting, and healthy snacks, as well as promoting a positive and supportive culture. I will make sure that my team members have access to comfortable seating, natural lighting, and healthy snacks, as well as a positive and supportive culture. By doing so, I will promote the well-being and balance of my team members, which will ultimately lead to increased productivity and job satisfaction. Today, I will provide a healthy and comfortable working environment to promote well-being and balance.

Today's Leadership Affirmation:

I am willing to make difficult decisions, when necessary, while still taking into consideration the input of my team members.

I am willing to make difficult decisions, when necessary, while still taking into consideration the input of my team members. I understand that leadership sometimes requires making difficult decisions. I strive to make these choices while still considering the input of my team members to minimize the negative impact on them. I will make difficult decisions when necessary while still taking into consideration the input of my team members. I recognize that effective leadership sometimes requires making tough choices. I commit to doing so while considering the perspectives of my team members to minimize the negative impact on them. I will prioritize making difficult decisions, when necessary, while still valuing the input of my team members. I understand that effective leadership sometimes requires difficult choices, and I will strive to

[108]

make these decisions with consideration for the well-being of my team.

Today's Leadership Affirmation:

I am a leader who is able to recognize and respond to the emotional needs of my team members in order to create a positive work culture.

I am a leader who is able to recognize and respond to the emotional needs of my team members in order to create a positive work culture. A good leader understands that their team members are not just employees but individuals with emotions, needs and aspirations. By recognizing and responding to their emotional needs, I can foster a positive work culture that supports and motivates them to perform at their best. I am aware being able to regulate one's emotions is essential for maintaining a positive and productive work environment, as well as for building strong relationships with team members and stakeholders. Today, I will prioritize recognizing and responding to the emotional needs of my team members in order to create a positive work culture. By taking the time to understand and address their emotional needs, I can help foster a positive work culture that supports the success of the team and the organization as a whole.

Today's Leadership Affirmation:

I am a leader who is able to provide my team members with a clear path to professional growth and advancement.

I am a leader who is able to provide my team members with a clear path to professional growth and advancement. Providing a clear path to professional growth and advancement is essential for retaining and motivating top talent. As a leader, I work to ensure that my team members have clear goals and opportunities, helping them to reach their full potential. I strive to identify the career aspirations of each team member and provide opportunities for growth and development, including mentoring and regular feedback. I believe that helping my team members achieve their career goals not only benefits them but also strengthens the team and drives the success of the organization. Today, I will find new opportunities to offer my team members, creating a clear path for growth and advancement.

Today's Leadership Affirmation:

I work with my team to identify and implement technology solutions that best fit the organization's needs.

I work with my team to identify and implement technology solutions that best fit the organization's needs. I believe in the power of teamwork and collaboration. I work closely with my team members to identify technology solutions that best fit the organization's needs. By involving my team in the process, I ensure that the solutions we implement are tailored to the organization's specific needs and that everyone is on board with the changes. I recognize the importance of involving my team in the decision-making process to ensure that the solutions we choose are the best fit for the organization's unique needs and goals. By working collaboratively, we can draw on each other's expertise and insights to identify the most effective technology solutions. This approach not only helps to streamline operations, increase efficiency, and drive growth, but also fosters a culture of teamwork and innovation within the organization.

Today's Leadership Affirmation:

I am a leader who is able to use emotional intelligence to build strong relationships with stakeholders and clients, promoting trust and respect.

I am a leader who is able to use emotional intelligence to build strong relationships with stakeholders and clients, promoting trust and respect. By using emotional intelligence, I am able to build strong relationships, promoting trust and respect. This helps me to connect with others on a deeper level, understand their perspectives and needs, and create mutually beneficial outcomes. By using emotional intelligence, I am able to connect with others on a deeper level, understand their perspectives and needs, and build strong relationships essential for successful partnerships and projects. Today, I will use emotional intelligence to build strong relationships with stakeholders and clients; I will work to promote trust and respect with those around me.

Today's Leadership Affirmation:

I am a leader who is able to maintain transparency in all aspects of the organization, including financial, operations, and strategy.

I am a leader who is able to maintain transparency in all aspects of the organization, including financial, operations, and strategy. This means that I understand the importance of being open and honest about the organization's financial and operational information. I make sure that everyone is aware of the organization's financial status, and that they have access to all relevant information. I will be a leader who maintains transparency in all aspects of the organization, including financial, operations, and strategy. I understand the importance of being open and honest about the organization's financial and operational information. Today, I will help build trust within the organization, and ensure that everyone is informed and aligned with the organization's goals and strategies.

Today's Leadership Affirmation:

I am a leader who is able to use critical thinking and problem-solving skills to analyze and evaluate information, identify the root cause of problems, and find solutions.

I am a leader who is able to use critical thinking and problem-solving skills to analyze and evaluate information, identify the root cause of problems, and find solutions. This means that I have the ability to analyze complex situations and find effective solutions, even in difficult or challenging circumstances. I use a systematic approach to problem-solving, and I am able to evaluate information, identify patterns and relationships, and make informed decisions. challenges and issues in a structured and analytical manner. I break down complex problems into smaller components, identify the root cause of the problem, and develop effective solutions to address it. Additionally, my ability to evaluate information, identify patterns and relationships, and make informed decisions allows our team to effectively navigate difficult or challenging situations and make well-informed choices. Today, I will approach problem-solving systematically, using a data-driven approach to identify patterns and relationships, and make informed decisions that benefit my team and the organization as a whole.

Today's Leadership Affirmation:

I am a leader who is able to navigate and lead in a diverse and multicultural environment.

I am a leader who is able to navigate and lead in a diverse and multicultural environment. I understand that working in a diverse environment can bring unique challenges, but I am able to effectively lead and communicate with team members from a variety of backgrounds and cultures. This allows me to effectively reach a wider audience and build a more inclusive workplace. As a leader, I recognize the importance of diversity and cultural understanding in today's global business landscape. I make it a priority to learn about different cultures and customs, and to create a work environment that is respectful and inclusive of all team members. This involves promoting open communication, encouraging diversity of thought and perspective, and implementing policies and practices that support cultural understanding and sensitivity. By leading in a diverse and multicultural environment, I am able to leverage the unique strengths and perspectives of my team members, and to build a more successful and innovative team.

Today's Leadership Affirmation:

I understand the importance of team members being informed and on the same page, and actively work to make sure they are aware of the reasons behind decisions.

I understand the importance of team members being informed and on the same page, and actively work to make sure they are aware of the reasons behind decisions. Effective leaders understand the importance of keeping their team members informed, and they actively work to ensure that everyone is aware of the reasons behind decisions. This approach helps to foster a sense of collaboration and teamwork, and it helps to increase accountability and ensure that everyone is working toward common goals. I understand that keeping my team members informed and on the same page is crucial for achieving success. By actively working to ensure that everyone is aware of the reasons behind decisions, I will create a more cohesive and productive team. This means communicating clearly and regularly, as well as being open to feedback and questions from team members.

When everyone is informed and on the same page, it is easier to work toward common goals and make decisions that benefit the team as a whole.

Today's Leadership Affirmation:

I am a transformational leader.

I am a transformational leader and I understand the importance of driving organizational change in order to achieve our strategic vision. Innovation can often require a significant investment of time and resources, but I understand the potential rewards. As a transformational leader, I understand the importance of communicating the need for change to my team and helping them to understand how it will benefit them and the organization as a whole. I will work to build buy-in and support for our transformational initiatives by engaging with team members and stakeholders at all levels of the organization. I understand that organizational change is essential for achieving long-term success and the need to constantly evaluate and adapt to meet the ever-changing needs of the market and our customers. Today, I will work to identify areas where we need to transform our organization and develop strategies for driving that change. I will hold myself and my team accountable for delivering results, and I will recognize and celebrate our successes along the way.

Today's Leadership Affirmation:

I understand the importance of clear and transparent communication, and actively work to improve it.

I understand the importance of clear and transparent communication, and actively work to improve it. Clear and transparent communication is crucial to the success of any team or organization. Thus, I work to improve my communication skills, ensuring that everyone is on the same page and working toward the same goals. I will prioritize improving my communication skills and making them clear and transparent, recognizing their importance in fostering a successful team or organization. I will actively seek out feedback from team members and work to address any areas of improvement. By doing so, I can build trust, respect, and collaboration within the team, ultimately leading to greater success and a more positive work environment.

REFLECTIONS ON LEADERSHIP PRINCIPLES

REFLECTIONS ON LEADERSHIP PRINCIPLES

Ask any leader to produce a list of principles or traits that a leader should aspire to and you will rarely get the same answer twice. Although, you will find certain traits that continuously arise that, to be effective, a leader must embody, such as Integrity, Emotional Intelligence, Communication, Resilience, and Self-confidence. Below is a collection of leadership self-development themes, their supporting affirmations and "I will" statements. As a leader, if you are planning on strengthening your skills in your foundational principles, these are a great place to start.

Continuous Improvement

Continuous improvement: I am a leader who is committed to continuous improvement. I am always seeking ways to improve my leadership skills, and I am dedicated to becoming the best leader I can be.

Leadership affirmation: I am a leader who is committed to continuous improvement. I recognize that there is always room for growth and development, and I am constantly seeking out opportunities to enhance my leadership skills.

I will statement: I will dedicate time and effort to actively seek out opportunities for professional development, such as attending leadership workshops or seeking feedback from colleagues. I will remain open to constructive criticism and use it as an opportunity to learn and grow. I will consistently reflect on my leadership practices and strive to implement new ideas and strategies to improve the success of my team and organization.

Decisiveness

Decisiveness: I am a leader who makes difficult decisions quickly and effectively. I trust my instincts, weigh all the options, and make decisions with confidence, knowing that my actions will lead to positive results.

Leadership affirmation: I am a decisive leader who makes tough decisions with confidence and clarity. I trust my instincts and am not afraid to take action when necessary.

I will statement: I will trust my instincts and make decisions confidently, even when faced with uncertainty or difficult choices. I will weigh all the options and act decisively, knowing that my leadership will drive positive results for my team and organization.

Emotional Intelligence

Emotional intelligence: I am a leader who possesses emotional intelligence and is able to understand and manage my own emotions as well as those of others. I use my emotional intelligence to build strong relationships and foster a positive work environment.

Emotional intelligence: I am a leader who understands and manages my own emotions and those of others. I use my emotional intelligence to build strong relationships, create a positive work environment, and make informed decisions.

Leadership affirmation: I am a leader who recognizes the importance of emotional intelligence and its impact on team dynamics. I understand and manage my emotions effectively and use my emotional intelligence to connect with my team and create a positive work environment.

I will statement: I will continue to develop my emotional intelligence by actively listening to my team, being aware of my own emotions, and using empathy to understand the emotions of others. I will also encourage my team to develop their emotional intelligence by creating an environment that values and supports emotional intelligence growth.

Communication Skills

Communication skills: I am a leader who effectively communicates information and ideas. I listen actively, speak clearly, and use my communication skills to build strong relationships, inspire others, build trust and create positive outcomes.

Leadership affirmation: My effective communication skills enable me to build strong relationships and foster a positive work environment. I am an excellent listener and communicator, and I use my skills to inspire and motivate my team to achieve their goals.

I will statement: I will continue to improve my communication skills by actively listening to my team members, providing feedback and clear instructions, and using appropriate body language and tone of voice. I will strive to create an open and transparent communication environment where everyone feels heard and understood.

Strategic Thinking

Strategic thinking: I am a leader who thinks about the long-term direction and performance of my organization. I use my strategic thinking skills to make informed decisions that drive success and improve performance.

Leadership affirmation: I am a leader who is skilled in strategic planning. I have a clear vision for the future of my organization, and I am committed to developing and executing strategies that will help us achieve our goals.

I will statement: I will use my strategic-planning skills to assess the needs of my organization and identify opportunities for growth and improvement. I will develop and implement strategies that align with our mission and values, and that help us to achieve our long-term objectives.

Adaptability

Adaptability: I am a leader who changes and adapts in response to new information and circumstances. I am flexible and open-minded, and I always seek new opportunities to learn and grow.

Leadership affirmation: I embrace change and am adaptable to new situations. I am open-minded and always looking for ways to learn and grow, which allows me to lead my team toward success.

I will statement: I will remain open-minded and flexible in my leadership approach, embracing change as an opportunity for growth. I will seek out new knowledge and perspectives, and use this information to make informed decisions that will lead my team toward success.

Resilience

Resilience: I am a leader who bounces back from adversity and setbacks. I have the strength and determination to overcome obstacles and stay focused on my goals, even in the face of adversity.

Leadership affirmation: I am a leader who bounces back from adversity and setbacks. I have the strength and determination to overcome obstacles and stay focused on my goals, even in the face of adversity.

I will statement: I will approach challenges with a positive attitude and a growth mindset. I will persevere through difficult times, remaining focused on my goals and staying determined to achieve success. I will seek out support from others when needed and remain resilient in the face of adversity.

Personal growth

Personal growth: I am a leader who is committed to personal growth and development. I am always seeking new opportunities to learn and improve, and I am dedicated to becoming the best version of myself.

Leadership affirmation: I am a leader who values personal growth and development. I am committed to continually learning and improving, and I understand that my personal growth will positively impact my team and organization.

I will statement: I will actively seek out opportunities for personal growth and development. I will set aside time for self-reflection and learning, and I will prioritize my own growth as a leader.

Self-awareness

Self-awareness: I am a leader who understands my own strengths and weaknesses, and how they impact others. I use my self-awareness to develop my leadership skills and improve my effectiveness as a leader.

Leadership affirmation: I am a leader who values self-awareness and strives to understand my impact on others. By investing time and effort into developing my self-awareness, I am able to lead with greater effectiveness and inspire my team to achieve their full potential.

I will statement: I will continue to prioritize my self-awareness as a leader by seeking out feedback and constructive criticism. I will actively listen to others and reflect on my own behavior to better understand my strengths and areas for improvement. By being more self-aware, I will lead my team with greater effectiveness and inspire them to reach their full potential.

Inspirational Leadership

Inspirational Leadership: I am a leader who inspires and motivates others to achieve a common goal. I have a clear vision and communicate it in a way that inspires and motivates others to take action.

Leadership affirmation: I am a leader who inspires and motivates others to achieve greatness. I am able to communicate my vision in a way that ignites passion and enthusiasm in my team, and I lead by example, setting the standard for excellence.

I will statement: I will continue to work on my communication skills to ensure that I am able to effectively convey my vision and inspire others. I will also lead by example, demonstrating the qualities that I want to see in my team, and provide support and encouragement to help them reach their full potential.

Integrity

Integrity: I am a leader who is honest and has strong moral principles. I always do the right thing, even when no one is watching, and my actions are guided by my values and principles.

Leadership affirmation: I lead with integrity, guided by strong moral principles and a commitment to doing what is right. My actions are always aligned with my values, and I inspire trust and respect from those around me.

I will statement: I will continue to uphold my integrity as a leader by always prioritizing honesty and doing what is right. I will hold myself accountable to my values and principles, and I will inspire my team to do the same.

AFTERWARD

My hope is that the collective affirmations found in this volume of work have enriched your life. Our world needs exceptional leaders. If I was able to contribute my thoughts and reflections toward your pursuit of becoming a leader who makes a difference in our world, then I am truly proud and humbled. While it is true that leadership as a discipline is not an easy endeavor, I will always believe that it is rewarding, and when done right - enlightening. May you achieve your life's pursuits and may you enrich others along the way.

Compiling these affirmations was a truly enjoyable exercise and I hope you have been able to gain some insight and support on your leadership journey, through their regular use in your developmental activities. Remember, using leadership affirmations can be a powerful tool for improving your mindset, boosting your confidence, and developing your leadership skills.

I like to use this book as a reference, revisiting the daily affirmations in random order to continue to introduce applicable concepts into my daily approach. You can adopt this approach or start at the beginning and work your way through the material again and again. As noted, using leadership affirmations can support your development by making leadership an integrated part of your daily approach to life. Remember to set a specific goal, choose a time and place, read and reflect, repeat and reinforce, take action, track your progress, and use the book as a reference.

Additionally, look for other volumes of work in this series which offer even more affirmations for you to incorporate into your growth. If you have enjoyed the journey so far – keep going, your inner leadership self-discovery, and life-long learning journey awaits. By incorporating daily affirmations into your leadership development, you can transform your leadership style and become the best version of yourself as a leader. Thank you for making a difference.

ADDITIONAL WORKS BY THE AUTHOR

Leading with Purpose: Daily Affirmations for Effective
Leadership

Vol. 1

ABOUT THE AUTHOR

Dr. John E. Roessler has made leadership a lifelong passion. He has over 30 years of experience leading teams of various sizes and overseeing discrete levels of responsibility, from leading combat operations to serving as a Federal Executive. Dr. Roessler is combat veteran, holds an MBA and DBA of Strategy and Innovation. As a servant leader, he thrives on helping others achieve their greatest successes.

www.ingramcontent.com/pod-product-compliance
Lightning Source LLC
Chambersburg PA
CBHW062109080426
42734CB00012B/2805